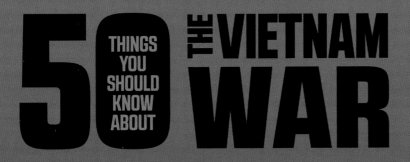

50
THINGS YOU SHOULD KNOW ABOUT
THE VIETNAM WAR

by Chris McNab

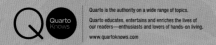

Quarto is the authority on a wide range of topics.
Quarto educates, entertains and enriches the lives of our readers—enthusiasts and lovers of hands-on living.
www.quartoknows.com

Publisher: Maxime Boucknooghe
Editorial Director: Victoria Garrard
Art Director: Miranda Snow
Design and Editorial: Tall Tree Ltd
Consultant: Andrew Wiest, University Distinguished Professor of History, The University of Southern Mississippi

Copyright © QEB Publishing, Inc. 2016

Published in the United States by
QEB Publishing, Inc.
6 Orchard Road
Lake Forest, CA 92630

A CIP record for this book is available from the Library of Congress.

ISBN 978 1 60992 961 9

Printed in China

Words in **bold** are explained in the glossary on page 78.

CONTENTS

INTRODUCTION

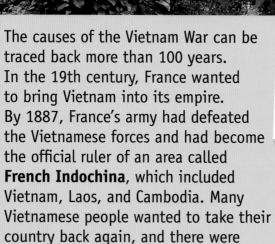

The Vietnam War was one of the longest conflicts in the history of the United States. America began sending small numbers of military advisors to the war in the 1950s, but by 1968 there were more than 500,000 soldiers in South Vietnam. The very last Americans did not leave there until 1975, by which time 58,286 U.S. troops were dead. But the war was far more devastating to Vietnam and its people. In total, the war may have cost up to one and a half million Vietnamese lives.

THE FRENCH TAKE OVER

The causes of the Vietnam War can be traced back more than 100 years. In the 19th century, France wanted to bring Vietnam into its empire. By 1887, France's army had defeated the Vietnamese forces and had become the official ruler of an area called **French Indochina**, which included Vietnam, Laos, and Cambodia. Many Vietnamese people wanted to take their country back again, and there were frequent rebellions against French rule.

◄ A propaganda poster from 1942 showing the French flag flying over Vietnam.

► French soldiers in the jungles of Vietnam during the conquest of the country in the 1880s.

From the mid-19th century until 1954, the official language of Vietnam was French.

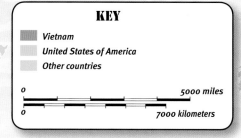

Map showing the locations of Vietnam and the United States.

UNITED STATES OF AMERICA

Pacific Ocean

KEY

Vietnam
United States of America
Other countries

0   5000 miles

0   7000 kilometers

▼ *Vietnam's lush jungles provided plenty of hiding spaces for soldiers during the war.*

VIETNAM'S LANDSCAPE AND WEATHER

Vietnam is a tropical country. In the summer months it is very hot and humid (the air feels damp), while in winter it is mild and even quite cold in the mountainous parts and in the north. It has periods of very heavy rain, and huge storms can batter the coast. Vietnam has different types of landscape, including thick jungles, high mountains, swamps, many rivers, rice-growing fields, beaches on the coast, and big cities such as Hanoi and Ho Chi Minh City (previously called Saigon).

AMERICA'S LONGEST CONFLICTS

VIETNAM — **18 YEARS**

AFGHANISTAN — **14 YEARS+**

IRAQ WAR **9 YEARS+**

AMERICAN REVOLUTION — **8 YEARS**

A region in turmoil

The United States was not the first foreign country to fight a major war in Vietnam. From 1946, France also battled against Vietnamese communists in a conflict known as the First Indochina War, which France lost in 1954.

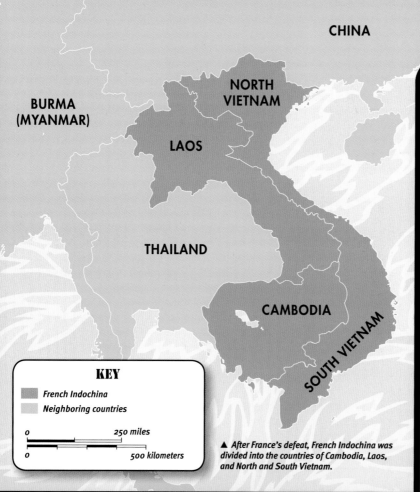

CHINA

NORTH VIETNAM

BURMA (MYANMAR)

LAOS

THAILAND

CAMBODIA

SOUTH VIETNAM

KEY

French Indochina

Neighboring countries

0   250 miles

0   500 kilometers

▲ After France's defeat, French Indochina was divided into the countries of Cambodia, Laos, and North and South Vietnam.

WHAT HAPPENED?

Before World War II, France ruled over a large colony in Southeast Asia known as French Indochina. This included what we now call Vietnam. During World War II, the Japanese occupied French Indochina. Japan was defeated in 1945, and France attempted to return to rule over Indochina, but communist forces fought a nine-year war from 1946 to 1954 to stop this happening.

Vietnam became independent in 938 AD after centuries of Chinese rule.

KEY EVENTS

October 1945
French forces return to Indochina after World War II (see above).

December 1946
The First Indochina War begins between France and communist forces. (see page 8).

October 1949
The communist People's Republic of China is established.

September 1950
The United States begins providing support to the French in Vietnam, Cambodia, and Laos.

▲ A defeated Japanese soldier salutes a French officer in Saigon, French Indochina, at the end of World War II.

COMMUNIST HELP

▲ One of hundreds of Soviet-built trucks sold to North Vietnam by China in the 1950s.

THE COLD WAR IN SOUTHEAST ASIA

Southeast Asia was a long way from both the United States and the **Soviet Union**. Both countries, however, wanted the region to be their ally and to adopt their philosophies of **communism** (Soviet Union and China) or **democracy** (United States). So the Soviet Union and China sent money, equipment, and weapons to communist groups and the United States sent money, equipment, and weapons to anti-communist government forces.

U.S. HELP

◀ As well as sending MAAG military advisors, the USA also sold planes and aircraft carriers to the French.

March–May 1954
France is defeated by communist forces at the Battle of Dien Bien Phu (see page 10).

April–July 1954
The Geneva Accords divide Vietnam into a communist North and a U.S.-backed South (see page 11).

February 1955
The USA establishes the Military Assistance Advisory Group (MAAG) to train South Vietnamese forces.

1956–63
Communist guerrillas fight the South Vietnamese army. U.S. support increases (see pages 12–13).

In total, China provided the Viet Minh with more than six million rounds of ammunition.

2

War against the French

▲ Pictured here near the end of his life, Vo Nguyen Giap died in 2013 aged 102.

The French forces were better equipped and armed than their opponent, the **Viet Minh**, which was largely a peasant army. However, the French underestimated the skill of the Viet Minh commander, Vo Nguyen Giap. From 1949, the newly created People's Republic of China supplied Giap with arms, and the French began to lose control of the Vietnamese countryside.

VO NGUYEN GIAP

The commander of the Viet Minh, Vo Nguyen Giap, is one of history's greatest generals. His **guerrilla** tactics effectively resisted three technologically superior occupiers: the Japanese in 1942–45, the French in 1946–54, and the Americans from 1965.

INDOCHINA WAR CASUALTIES

✸ FRANCE:
75,581 dead
64,127 wounded

40,000 taken prisoner

✸ VIETNAMESE CIVILIANS:
Up to 400,000 dead

✸ VIET MINH:
Up to 300,000 dead

▼ Franco-Vietnamese medics treat a wounded Viet Minh POW in 1954.

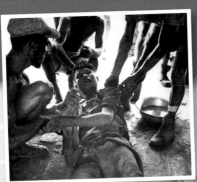

◄ Followed by a tank donated by the USA, a French soldier marches through Vietnam near the end of the French-Indochina War.

Ho Chi Minh

Ho Chi Minh was the leader of the Vietnamese communist forces, and became leader of North Vietnam after the defeat of the French. Known as "Uncle Ho" to his people, he was clever, ruthless, and very patient, believing that victory would come with time. He died in 1969, six years before North Vietnam's final victory over South Vietnam.

> "You will kill 10 of our men, and we will kill one of yours, and in the end it will be you who tire of it."
> – Ho Chi Minh, 1946

▲ Before he returned to Vietnam in 1941, Ho Chi Minh had spent 30 years abroad, working and studying in France, England, China, and the Soviet Union.

3

THE VIET MINH

Formed in 1941, the Viet Minh was a communist guerrilla force dedicated to overthrowing its colonial occupiers. Its armed units became known as the People's Army of Vietnam (PAVN). The Viet Minh spread throughout Vietnamese society. Some units were made up of just a few men in a village, while others had thousands of soldiers.

▲ The Viet Minh flag, shown here, is now used as the official flag of Vietnam.

4 ▶ Dien Bien Phu

Dien Bien Phu is in northwest Vietnam. It is a valley surrounded by high, jungle-covered mountains. French forces occupied the valley in 1953. Their commander, Christian de Castries, hoped to draw the Viet Minh out and destroy them in open battle. Instead, his men became trapped in a violent siege that ended in defeat.

◀ The French were equipped with a number of U.S.-made M24 Chaffee light tanks, which, for a while, succeeded in repelling the Viet Minh attacks.

WHAT HAPPENED?

The Viet Minh used bicycles, animals, and human strength to carry hundreds of artillery guns into the surrounding mountains. From there they began shelling the French positions down below, and fired at French aircraft trying to bring in supplies. They also moved soldiers closer to the French positions by digging tunnels. The French soldiers were trapped, and on May 7, 1954, the surviving 12,000 French troops surrendered.

▲ De Castries studies his battle plans in a bunker in Dien Bien Phu.

◄ This 1954 map shows the French positions in the valley. From the surrounding hills, the Viet Minh could clearly see the French soldiers below to aim their weapons at them.

FRENCH COMMANDER

General Christian de Castries was the French commander who oversaw the defeat at Dien Bien Phu that more or less ended the French-Indochina war. He was taken prisoner after Dien Bien Phu and held for four months while peace negotiations took place.

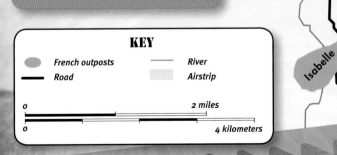

Gabrielle

Anne-Marie

Huguette

Beatrice

Dominique

Eliane

Claudine

Nam Yum River

Isabelle

▶ French troops take cover from the shelling in trenches.

THE FRENCH FORTIFICATIONS

The French created a headquarters and a series of outposts at Dien Bien Phu. Each outpost consisted of trenches, sandbag positions, barbed wire, and heavily armed French soldiers. The outposts were all given girls' names, such as "Beatrice" and "Isabelle." The Viet Minh captured or destroyed each outpost one by one.

KEY

French outposts	River
Road	Airstrip

0   2 miles

0   4 kilometers

NORTH VIETNAM

★ Dien Bien Phu

THE GENEVA ACCORDS

Once the French were defeated, Vietnam was divided into two halves by an agreement called the **Geneva Accords**. The northern part of the country (North Vietnam) was communist, and led by Ho Chi Minh. The southern part (South Vietnam) was supported by the United States, and led by Ngo Dinh Diem.

SOUTH VIETNAM

▲ North Vietnamese officials (closest to the camera) argue their case before the signing of the Geneva Accords on July 21, 1954.

KEY

North Vietnam	0 300 miles
South Vietnam	0 600 kilometers

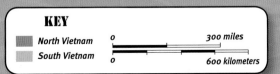

11

Problems in the South

5

NORTH VIETNAM

900,000 people

100,000 people

SOUTH VIETNAM

The Geneva Accords stated that North and South Vietnam would hold elections in 1956 to unify the country. These did not happen. Instead, from 1960 onward, a communist force called the **Viet Cong (VC)** launched guerrilla attacks in South Vietnam. The South tried to fight back, but many civilians were killed. South Vietnam seemed to be losing control.

▼ *Hundreds of anti-communist Vietnamese wait for the U.S.S. Montague to take them to South Vietnam in August 1954.*

POPULATION MOVEMENTS

After the Geneva Accords, huge migrations took place within Vietnam. Up to 100,000 Viet Minh moved to the communist-controlled north. More than 900,000 Catholic and anti-communist Vietnamese moved south.

THE DOMINO THEORY

At this time, many politicians believed that if one country fell to communism, the country next to it would fall to communism as well—like dominoes falling into one another. This idea was called the "domino theory," and the United States believed it had to step in to stop the process in Asia.

The Americans get involved

6

▲ The government of South Vietnam tried to protect its citizens by moving them to fortified areas called "strategic hamlets," like this one.

President John F. Kennedy feared the spread of communism in the world. In 1961, he told a news reporter that "Vietnam is the place" where America had to show its power to stop communism. He began sending money, equipment, and military advisors to South Vietnam to help fight the enemy.

JOHN F. KENNEDY

An idealistic young politician, John F. Kennedy took a firm stand against communism when he became U.S. President in 1961. As well as trying to stop the spread of communism in Southeast Asia, he also tried (and failed) to overthrow the new communist government of Fidel Castro in Cuba.

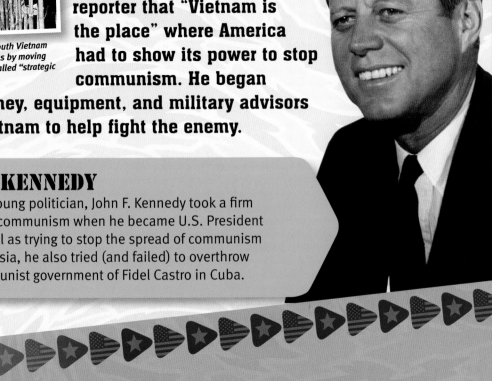

Kennedy believed that he would never be re-elected if he lost Vietnam to the communists.

TOTAL AMERICAN COST OF SUPPORTING SOUTH VIETNAM 1960–65

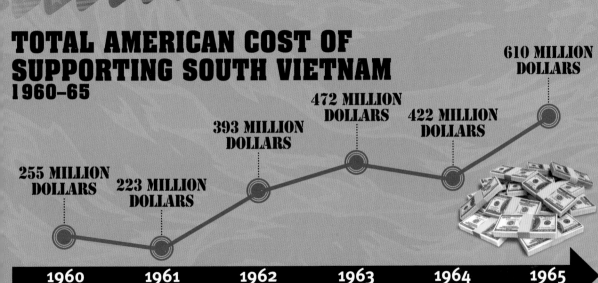

255 MILLION DOLLARS

223 MILLION DOLLARS

393 MILLION DOLLARS

472 MILLION DOLLARS

422 MILLION DOLLARS

610 MILLION DOLLARS

| 1960 | 1961 | 1962 | 1963 | 1964 | 1965 |

7 1963–1967

A superpower war

When John F. Kennedy became President in 1961, there were 800 U.S. military advisors in South Vietnam. When it became clear that South Vietnam's army, the **ARVN**, was struggling to beat the Viet Cong, he began to send more American troops to help. By the end of 1962, the number had risen to more than 11,000.

▼ *President Johnson is greeted enthusiastically by troops during a visit to Vietnam in 1966. By that time, he had growing doubts about the war, privately believing that it would turn out badly for the USA.*

WHAT HAPPENED?

In 1963, President Kennedy was **assassinated** and President Lyndon Johnson took over. It was Johnson who transformed the conflict in Vietnam into a major U.S. war. From 1961 to 1965, most American troops served as trainers for the Army of the Republic of Vietnam (ARVN), although some "Green Beret" **special forces** joined the South Vietnamese troops on combat missions. However, from 1965 Johnson openly sent U.S. combat troops to fight against the Viet Cong.

KEY EVENTS

January 2, 1963
ARVN forces, with U.S. advisors, are defeated by the Viet Cong during the battle of Ap Bac.

November 2, 1963
Ngo Dinh Diem is overthrown and murdered (see page 15).

November 22, 1963
President John F. Kennedy is assassinated. Lyndon Johnson takes over (see above).

August 7, 1964
The Gulf of Tonkin Resolution is passed (see page 20).

NGO DINH DIEM (1901–1963)

Ngo Dinh Diem was the first President of South Vietnam. However, his dictatorial behavior and discrimination against the country's Buddhists made many in the South hate him. It also made the Viet Cong, who fought against him, more popular. Diem was assassinated on November 2, 1963, and was replaced by military commander Tuong Van Minh.

▼ *Diem came to power in 1955. He claimed that 98 percent of people voted for him.*

▲ *President Kennedy smiles at the crowds in Dallas, just moments before the assassin's first bullet hits him.*

THE ASSASSINATION OF JOHN F. KENNEDY

On Friday, November 22, 1963, President Kennedy visited Dallas, Texas, to rally support for his 1964 presidential bid. The country waited to see what he would do in Vietnam. Three weeks previously, the unpopular president of South Vietnam, Ngo Dinh Diem, had been assassinated and the country had become extremely unstable, with growing support for the Viet Cong. There was little appetite in Washington to commit combat troops to Vietnam. However, the **CIA** warned Kennedy that the Viet Cong were intensifying their efforts. At this key moment, the president was killed in Dallas by a lone assassin, Lee Harvey Oswald, whose motives were unclear.

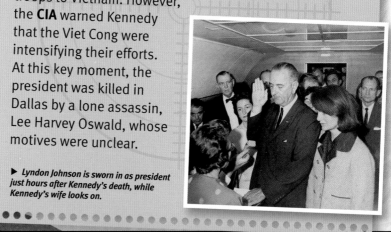

▶ *Lyndon Johnson is sworn in as president just hours after Kennedy's death, while Kennedy's wife looks on.*

March, 1965
Operation *Rolling Thunder* begins and the first U.S ground troops arrive (see pages 24–26).

September 3, 1967
Nguyen Van Thieu is elected President of South Vietnam. There are now 385,000 U.S. troops in the country.

January 30, 1968
North Vietnam launches the Tet Offensive, an attack on South Vietnam (see pages 36–37).

November 1968
Richard Nixon is elected U.S. President (see page 44).

The Viet Cong

Viet Cong was the name given by Western troops to communist guerrillas fighting the government in South Vietnam. They actually called themselves the National Liberation Front (NLF). Viet Cong soldiers wore black cotton clothing and rubber sandals cut from car tires. Many were experts in jungle warfare, and preferred ambushes, bombings, and **booby traps** to open battles.

◀ *This guerrilla fighter wears the Viet Cong's characteristic floppy jungle hat and carries a Type-56 assault rifle.*

▲ *The flag of the Viet Cong was the flag of North Vietnam, but with a blue stripe added.*

Viet Cong would often wear peasant clothes, so U.S. troops could not tell friend from foe.

▲ *North Vietnamese carry supplies to Viet Cong fighters in the South along the Ho Chi Minh trail, which ran through Laos.*

VIET CONG ORGANIZATION

The Viet Cong was organized into full-time fighters and part-time soldiers who served in villages and other local areas. They were supported by thousands of civilians, who provided the soldiers with food, shelter, and information. Any civilians who refused to support the Viet Cong could be threatened with murder.

VIET CONG WEAPONS

Viet Cong forces were equipped by the Soviet Union and China. Most of the weapons were handheld and ideal for guerrilla fighting. Very few heavy artillery guns or tanks were used.

TYPE-56 RIFLE
Purpose: A Chinese copy of the Soviet AK-47.

RPG-7
Purpose: A rocket launcher that could destroy a tank.

HAND GRENADES
Purpose: Small bombs that could be thrown about 30 feet.

TUNNELS

The Viet Cong often used tunnel systems to hide from the enemy forces. The tunnels could be hundreds of feet long, and contained chambers for special activities.

◀ *U.S. "tunnel rats" explore a captured Viet Cong tunnel. This was risky work as the tunnels were often booby trapped, or crawling with poisonous snakes.*

BOOBY TRAPS

The Viet Cong were masters at setting booby traps. A booby trap is a device designed to kill or injure a person when it is set off by the victim. Viet Cong booby traps were everywhere. They included hidden pits filled with sharpened sticks, swinging balls of spikes, and hand grenades tied to trip wires. These devices killed hundreds of soldiers.

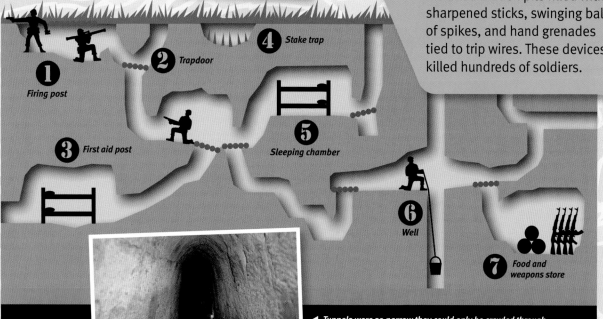

❶ Firing post

❷ Trapdoor

❹ Stake trap

❸ First aid post

❺ Sleeping chamber

❻ Well

❼ Food and weapons store

◀ *Tunnels were so narrow they could only be crawled through. They might lead to chambers for sleeping or storing weapons.*

North Vietnamese Army

The North Vietnamese Army (**NVA**) was the main military force of North Vietnam. Although the earlier army, the Viet Minh, had won victory over the French, the NVA realized that it could never defeat American forces in open battle. It still inflicted serious casualties on U.S. troops, however, and launched several major invasions of South Vietnam.

SUPPORT FROM THE SOVIETS

From around 1964, the Soviet Union sent its own military advisors to North Vietnam to train the NVA and the North Vietnamese Air Force (NVAF). Although many of the details are still secret, historians believe that about 3,000 Soviet advisors were in North Vietnam by 1965.

▼ *North Vietnamese pose with a Soviet-made missile launcher.*

▼ *A North Vietnamese soldier in 1966. He is armed with a submachine gun from World War II.*

NVA BELIEFS

The NVA soldiers were taught to believe the following:

★

There has been a revolution in Vietnam, but only in one half of the country.

★

North Vietnam has to free South Vietnam.

★

The NVA soldier must fight to liberate South Vietnam without questioning orders.

★

The NVA soldier must be prepared to face hardship and death.

The ARVN

As discussions of the Vietnam War tend to focus on the USA, the army of the Republic of Vietnam (ARVN) is often overlooked. Its soldiers were armed and equipped by the USA, but they had some poor leaders and often failed to perform well in combat. There were about 200,000 U.S. casualties during the war compared with more than a million ARVN ones.

▲ The flag of the Army of the Republic of Vietnam from 1955 to 1975. The army was disbanded at the end of the war.

▶ ARVN recruits practice using US-made M16 rifles. Many ARVN soldiers would not survive the war.

Around 3.3% of the South Vietnamese population was serving in the ARVN at any one time.

19

ARVN DEAD 1961–72

1961–65	30,427
1966	11,953
1967	12,716
1968	28,800
1969	22,000
1970	23,000
1971	19,901
1972	25,787

LIFE IN ARVN

Life for the ARVN soldier was very hard. The money they were paid was often so little that they had to ask American troops for rice to feed themselves. There was a lot of bullying, and many officers were not skilled soldiers, even though they had to lead men. Some ARVN troops deserted to the communists— although some communists also switched sides.

A U.S. Congress report in 2005 said the Gulf of Tonkin attack of August 4 never happened.

Gulf of Tonkin incident

On August 2, 1964, the American warship U.S.S. *Maddox* was attacked by North Vietnamese torpedo boats in the Gulf of Tonkin, off the coast of North Vietnam. Two days later, another U.S. Navy ship called U.S.S. *C. Turner Joy* also reported attacks. Angered by these incidents, the **U.S. Congress** passed the Gulf of Tonkin **Resolution**, which enabled the United States to go to war.

NORTH VIETNAM

Gulf of Tonkin

HAINAN

LAOS

THAILAND

KEY
North Vietnam
South Vietnam
Neighboring countries

0   250 miles
0   450 kilometers

SOUTH VIETNAM

CAMBODIA

★ Bien Hoa

WHAT HAPPENED?

✹ U.S.S. *MADDOX*: attacked by three torpedo boats, but retaliated by sinking one and damaging another with gunfire.

✹ U.S.S. *C. TURNER JOY*: reported being assaulted by five boats. After the war, however, it was revealed that the ship hadn't been attacked at all. The five enemy boats were simply meaningless "blips" on a radar screen.

GULF OF TONKIN RESOLUTION

The Gulf of Tonkin Resolution stated that the United States could "take all necessary steps, including the use of armed force," to defend the freedom of any state in Southeast Asia. This meant that President Lyndon Johnson could now send U.S. ground troops to fight in Vietnam.

▲ The U.S.S. C. Turner Joy *spent all of its naval career patrolling the Pacific Ocean.*

▲ The U.S.S. Maddox *was a destroyer that saw service in World War II, Korea, and Vietnam.*

The attacks escalate

By July 1964, 200 Americans and thousands of South Vietnamese had died in communist ambushes and acts of terrorism. Bombs exploded frequently on the streets of Saigon. American bases, such as those at Nam Don and Bien Hoa, came under attack from Viet Cong and NVA troops. President Johnson chose to strike back with more firepower.

BATTLE OF BIEN HOA

On November 1, 1964, Viet Cong troops made a surprise night attack on the American airbase and camp at Bien Hoa. The Viet Cong struck with artillery and explosives. Four Americans were killed, 19 wounded, and six American *B-57 Canberra* bombers were destroyed.

Between 1956 and 1959, only four Americans were killed in Vietnam.

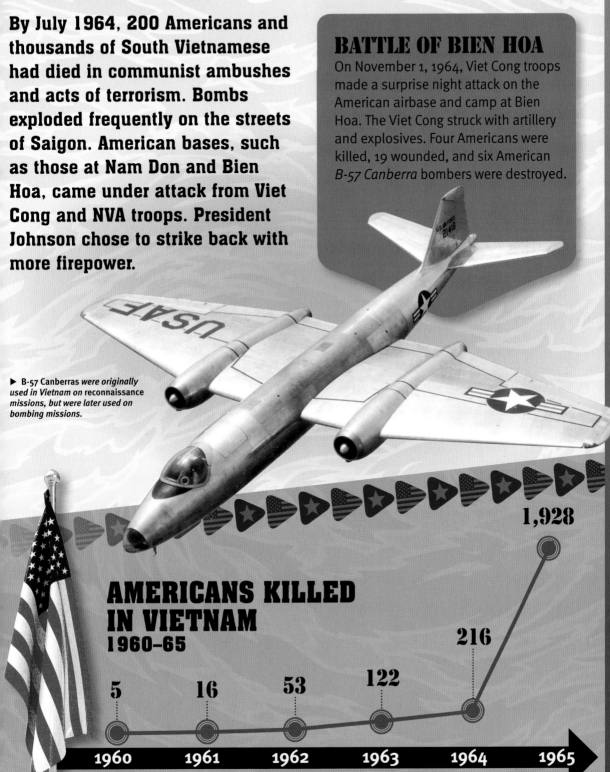

▶ B-57 Canberras *were originally used in Vietnam on* reconnaissance missions, but were later used on bombing missions.

AMERICANS KILLED IN VIETNAM
1960–65

1960	1961	1962	1963	1964	1965
5	16	53	122	216	1,928

13 ▶ The U.S. Navy

The U.S. Navy was vital to the American war effort in Vietnam. The roles they performed ranged from stopping and searching Vietnamese merchant ships for weapons, to launching massive air attacks against North Vietnam from enormous aircraft carriers.

▶ The U.S.S. America *was a Kitty Hawk Class carrier that served in Vietnam. It could carry nearly 80 aircraft and had a crew of more than 5,000 officers and men.*

CARRIER OPERATIONS

American aircraft carriers were the most powerful warships in the world. During the war, they were sent to two points off the Vietnamese coast, called Yankee Station and Dixie Station. Their aircraft flew missions from these stations. By 1968, carrier aircraft were making 6,000 combat flights a month.

▲ *The insignia (badge) of the U.S. Air Force is featured on all its planes.*

IMPORTANT U.S. CARRIER AIRCRAFT

Aircraft carriers can launch a range of aircraft to perform different roles. These are two of the most important aircraft used by the U.S. Navy during the Vietnam War.

GRUMMAN E-2C HAWKEYE

Purpose: Electronic **surveillance** aircraft
Maximum speed: 294 mph
Weapons: None, but its circular radar antenna was used to detect enemy aircraft.

MCDONNELL DOUGLAS F-4E PHANTOM II

Purpose: Enemy aircraft interceptor and ground-attack aircraft
Maximum speed: 1,472 mph
Weapons: Six-barrel gun; air-to-air missiles; air-to-ground missiles; rocket pods; bombs.

THE *FORRESTAL* INCIDENT

On July 29, 1967, the carrier U.S.S. *Forrestal* was on operations in the Gulf of Tonkin. At 10:50 a.m., a missile was accidentally fired from an aircraft on the flight deck. The missile caused a huge fire. Aircraft bombs and missiles began to explode as they cooked in the flames. By the time the fire was under control, 134 people had been killed and 161 injured.

▲ Fire crews hose down the blaze on the flight deck of the U.S.S. Forrestal.

▼ The U.S.S. New Jersey fires at targets near the Vietnamese coast in 1969.

U.S.S. *NEW JERSEY*

The U.S.S. *New Jersey* was the only American battleship sent to serve in the Vietnam War. The ship used its huge guns to pound enemy targets along the Vietnamese coastline. During a total of 120 days in combat, the ship fired nearly 20,000 artillery shells.

The American troop build-up

President Lyndon Johnson quickly realized that he would need large numbers of soldiers in Vietnam to fight the communists. Thousands were sent to South Vietnam, including many who were **drafted**. They were civilians who had been randomly chosen to serve in the armed forces.

NUMBERS OF U.S. TROOPS IN VIETNAM 1965–1972

Year	Troops
1965	184,300
1966	385,300
1967	485,600
1968	536,100
1969	475,200
1970	334,600
1971	156,800
1972	24,200

▶ American aircraft drop supplies for U.S. troops during February 1967.

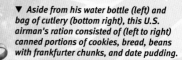

▼ Aside from his water bottle (left) and bag of cutlery (bottom right), this U.S. airman's ration consisted of (left to right) canned portions of cookies, bread, beans with frankfurter chunks, and date pudding.

U.S. LOGISTICS

To fight the war in Vietnam, American troops needed millions of tons of supplies every day. Most of the supplies were delivered by ships, and on any day there would be about 3,000 American supply ships in South Vietnamese ports. Many of these ships had traveled more than 7,000 miles from the United States.

The American soldier

15

▼ Most U.S. soldiers in Vietnam were young men, such as this teenage private pictured in 1965.

American troops in Vietnam were the best-trained and best-equipped soldiers in the world. The typical age of a soldier in Vietnam was 19–22, and for many of them this was their first trip abroad. They had to get used to a place completely unlike home.

WEAPONS OF THE U.S. INFANTRYMAN

M16 RIFLE
A light rifle that fired a bullet at a speed of 3,000 feet a second

M60 MACHINE GUN
Called "the Pig" by U.S. troops, because it was difficult to handle

M79 GRENADE LAUNCHER
A weapon that fired a small bomb to a distance of 430 yards

M18 CLAYMORE MINE
When triggered, the Claymore fired about 700 steel balls at the enemy

U.S. MARINE CORPS

The U.S. Marine Corps is a branch of the American armed services, and is part of the Navy rather than the Army. It is skilled in operations at sea, but in Vietnam it was used mainly as an elite infantry force. During the war, 57 marines won the Medal of Honor, the highest military award of the United States.

▶ Recently arrived U.S. marines ride in an M50 Ontos, a fast-moving antitank vehicle, across a Vietnam beach in 1965.

One U.S. bomb, known as "Walleye," had a TV camera in its nose to guide it to its target.

Rolling Thunder

From 1965 to 1968, the United States attacked North Vietnam in one of the biggest aircraft bombing campaigns in history—Operation *Rolling Thunder*. The goal was to force North Vietnam to stop sending supplies to Viet Cong troops in South Vietnam. The targets for the raids were chosen directly by the U.S. government in Washington, D.C.

70162

▲ *The B-52 Stratofortress was introduced in the 1950s and is still in active service today.*

WHAT HAPPENED?

During Operation *Rolling Thunder*, U.S. aircraft dropped more explosives on North Vietnam than were dropped on Germany and Japan during World War II. Aircraft flew a total of 304,000 sorties (individual aircraft missions). They hit targets like power stations, bridges, radars, and factories. *Rolling Thunder*, however, was a failure, and did not stop supplies getting through to the Viet Cong.

▶ *A U.S. Navy Grumman A-6 Intruder drops its bombs on Viet Cong positions as part of Operation Rolling Thunder.*

▲ The North Vietnamese MiG-15 was outdated by the start of the Vietnam War and was no match for modern U.S. jet fighters.

MIG vs PHANTOM

Over North Vietnam, U.S. *F-4 Phantoms* fought with enemy *MiG-15*, *MiG-17*, and *MiG-21* aircraft in fast air battles. During the war, *F-4 Phantoms* shot down more MiGs than any other U.S. aircraft, destroying 55 of them.

SURVIVING THE AIR RAIDS

To protect its population from the bombing, North Vietnam did the following:

✸ Built more than 21 million one-person air raid shelters to protect civilians living in cities.

✸ Evacuated 800,000 people from Hanoi.

✸ Stored engine oil in drums all around the countryside to keep it away from key city targets.

✸ Used 600,000 Vietnamese citizens to repair damage.

SURFACE-TO-AIR MISSILES

The North Vietnamese defended themselves against the American aircraft using a Soviet-made surface-to-air missile (**SAM**) called the *SA-2 Guideline*. In 1965, 194 SAMs were fired, but in 1967 this had escalated to 3,484. The North Vietnamese also had more than 7,000 anti-aircraft guns. In total, the Americans lost nearly 1,000 aircraft during *Rolling Thunder*.

◀ SA-2 Guideline *missiles could hit targets flying at an altitude of 82,000 feet.*

The Battle of Ia Drang Valley

Between November 14–18, 1965, American forces fought an epic battle against North Vietnamese Army (NVA) troops in the Ia Drang Valley. It was the first time U.S. soldiers had faced NVA units.

KEY

South Vietnam

Major battle

0   150 miles

0   300 kilometers

Ia Drang Valley

SOUTH VIETNAM

Saigon ★

▼ U.S. troops advance very carefully toward the enemy in the Ia Drang Valley.

◄ The Viet Cong had already won control of the rural Ia Drang area when the NVA moved in to support them, threatening Allied forces in the area.

WHAT HAPPENED?

American soldiers became locked in a fight for survival. At one point, 450 U.S. troops of the 1st Air Cavalry had to defend themselves against attacks from more than 2,000 NVA soldiers. On one day alone, 155 Americans were killed. In the end, however, American firepower pushed the NVA back over the border, and the communists lost more than 3,000 men.

U.S. AIRMOBILE TACTICS

▲ A transport helicopter lifts off after delivering U.S. soldiers on a mission in Ia Drang Valley.

The American forces became expert in "airmobile" tactics, which meant using helicopters to move soldiers around the battlefield. Attack helicopters might first fire rockets and machine guns to clear a "landing zone" (LZ). Then transport helicopters would fly troops into the LZ and special heavy-lift helicopters would keep the troops supplied.

Operation Cedar Falls

Operation *Cedar Falls* on January 8–26, 1967, was one of the biggest American and ARVN **search and destroy** missions of the Vietnam War. It was launched against Viet Cong troops in an area called the "Iron Triangle," and lasted nearly three weeks.

WHAT HAPPENED?

The U.S. and ARVN soldiers used a "hammer and anvil" tactic, trapping the VC between two forces. Areas of jungle were cleared of the VC and their underground tunnel bases destroyed. Entire enemy-controlled villages were wiped out with heavy plough machinery. By the time the operation finished, 750 VC and NVA troops had been killed and 250 captured. However, many Viet Cong still remained in the area.

▼ American tanks drive between dense jungle and fields of rubber plantations in Operation *Cedar Falls*.

THE IRON TRIANGLE

The Iron Triangle was located in Binh Duong Province, in the southern half of South Vietnam, to the north of Saigon. It was a major stronghold for the Viet Cong and North Vietnamese Army, who hid out in the thick jungles. The communist troops also built hundreds of miles of underground tunnels.

KEY

▨ Jungle	—— River
➤ U.S. attacks	--- Iron Triangle

0   5 miles

0   8 kilometers

▲ U.S. troops attacked the Viet Cong jungle stronghold simultanously from all sides in what was the largest ground operation of the entire war.

To get rid of the Viet Cong, U.S. troops often destroyed whole villages and areas of forest.

Search and destroy

"Search and destroy" was the main American tactic used against enemy forces in South Vietnam between 1965 and 1968. It involved U.S. troops searching villages and jungle for the enemy. Once found, they would attempt to destroy any enemy bases with massive firepower.

WHAT HAPPENED?

Search and destroy operations resulted in some major battles, but also thousands of small fights between American, South Vietnamese, and communist forces. American units were often ambushed and men were killed by booby traps. The U.S. soldiers often burned down villages that were suspected of sheltering Viet Cong troops. These attacks were known as "Zippo raids," after the popular brand of cigarette lighter used to light the fires.

Around 6,500 U.S. troops were killed by mines, booby traps, and other hidden devices.

MAJOR U.S. SEARCH AND DESTROY OPERATIONS

OPERATION *ATTELBORO*

Date: September 14–November 24, 1966
Purpose: Destroy communist forces in War Zone C, Tay Ninh Province
VC/NVA casualties: 2,278 killed; 34 prisoners
U.S. casualties: 282 killed; 1,576 wounded
ARVN casualties: Unknown

OPERATION *JUNCTION CITY*

Date: February 22–May 14, 1967
Purpose: Destroy communist forces near Dau Tieng, Binh Duong Province
VC/NVA casualties: 2,130 killed; 44 prisoners
U.S. casualties: 155 killed; 494 wounded
ARVN casualties: Unknown

THE LANDSCAPE

American combat soldiers in Vietnam often had to fight in dense jungles. They used machetes to cut their way through thick branches and vines just to walk a few feet. Venomous snakes and spiders were a constant danger, as well as the enemy. At night, mosquitoes and other biting insects would make life a misery.

▼ *A U.S soldier walks past the burning remains of a suspected Viet Cong base.*

CIVILIAN IRREGULAR DEFENSE GROUPS (CIDGS)

American special forces trained groups of South Vietnamese villagers to fight the Viet Cong. These groups were called Civilian Irregular Defense Groups (**CIDGs**). They were trained for about two weeks, and provided with American weapons and equipment. By late 1968, there were about 48,000 men in the CIDGs.

▲ *Members of a CIDG unit receive training.*

The Ho Chi Minh Trail

The **Ho Chi Minh Trail** was not a single track, but a vast network of supply routes leading from North Vietnam into South Vietnam. It ran through the jungles of Laos and Cambodia, which were Vietnam's neighbors, for a total distance of about 12,430 miles.

▼ Map showing the mountain passes along the trail connecting Laos and Cambodia with Vietnam.

NORTH VIETNAM

Nape Pass
Mu Gia Pass
Ban Karai Pass
DMZ

LAOS

THAILAND

CAMBODIA

SOUTH VIETNAM

★ Saigon

KEY
North Vietnam
South Vietnam
Neighboring countries
- → Ho Chi Minh Trail

0   300 miles
0   550 kilometers

◀ The trail meandered up and down steep banks, where ladders were used.

▼ Bicycles were used as carts to transport supplies along the trail.

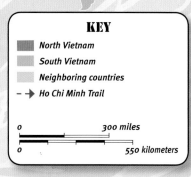

LIFE ON THE TRAIL

Tens of thousands of North Vietnamese soldiers and civilian workers moved supplies along the Ho Chi Minh Trail. The difficult landscape meant that while some supplies were carried in trucks, much was carried by people and animals. Thousands of bicycles were also used. Those who lived on the trail had to endure the hardships of the jungle and the threat of daily heavy bombing by the U.S. and ARVN air forces.

U.S. SURVEILLANCE

The Americans kept a constant watch on the Ho Chi Minh Trail. They used special cameras mounted to high-altitude aircraft to watch the trail night and day. They also used a device called an Air Delivered Seismic Intruder Device (ADSID). This looked like a bomb, but when dropped from an aircraft it buried itself in the ground and had an antenna sticking out, which was disguised as a branch. The device would detect the noises of nearby enemy troops and vehicles, and transmit their location to a listening post.

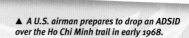
▲ A U.S. airman prepares to drop an ADSID over the Ho Chi Minh trail in early 1968.

◄ Many of the local trail watchers hired by the Americans to monitor the trail could not read or write. This device has pictograms to represent troops, trucks, and men that could be set to a number.

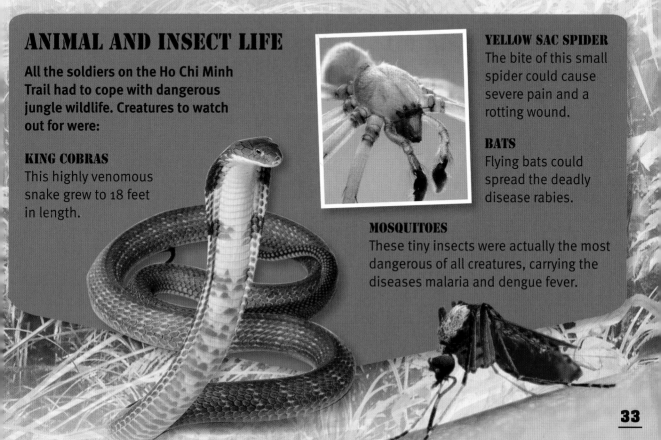

ANIMAL AND INSECT LIFE

All the soldiers on the Ho Chi Minh Trail had to cope with dangerous jungle wildlife. Creatures to watch out for were:

KING COBRAS
This highly venomous snake grew to 18 feet in length.

YELLOW SAC SPIDER
The bite of this small spider could cause severe pain and a rotting wound.

BATS
Flying bats could spread the deadly disease rabies.

MOSQUITOES
These tiny insects were actually the most dangerous of all creatures, carrying the diseases malaria and dengue fever.

1968–1970

The communist offensive

The years 1968–1970 marked a turning point in the Vietnam War. In 1968, the North Vietnamese launched a massive attack into South Vietnam called the **Tet Offensive**. It was defeated by U.S. and ARVN forces. But the strength of the attack, and the unpopularity of the war, led to the U.S. government beginning to withdraw its troops from South Vietnam.

▲ *Women search through wreckage caused by a Viet Cong bomb in 1968.*

▶ *The ruins of a motorbike lie on the street after a Viet Cong attack.*

VIET CONG ACTIVITIES

By the time of the Tet Offensive, the Viet Cong was killing or kidnapping hundreds of people every week:

1966–1969

■ Government workers   ■ Civilians

1,045   24,862
Kidnapped by Viet Cong

3,016   15,015
Murdered by Viet Cong

KEY EVENTS

January 30, 1968
The North Vietnamese launch the Tet Offensive (see pages 36–37).

May 3, 1968
President Johnson agrees to peace talks with North Vietnam, which begin informally.

May 10, 1968
Official peace talks begin in Paris (see page 62).

October 31, 1968
President Johnson announces that he will stop bombing North Vietnam.

NORTH VIETNAM

LAOS

Demilitarized Zone (DMZ)

Ben Hai River

Gio Linh

Con Thien

I McNamara Line

Cua Viet River

Cam Lo

Dong Ha

Quang Tri

Ca Lu

SOUTH VIETNAM

Lang Vei

Khe Sanh

Quang Tri River

▲ Map showing the Demilitarized Zone, McNamara Line, and U.S. military bases.

THE MCNAMARA LINE

Between the border of North and South Vietnam was a strip of land called the Demilitarized Zone (**DMZ**). Created in 1956, it was meant to be an area free from soldiers. During the Vietnam War, however, North Vietnamese forces regularly crossed the DMZ. In an attempt to stop them, the USA built a network of barriers with electronic surveillance devices along the DMZ. It was called the McNamara Line, after the U.S. Secretary of Defense, Robert McNamara. After a heavy attack by Viet Cong forces in 1968, the line was abandoned.

SAIGON

The capital of South Vietnam was Saigon. As well as being home to millions of people, it was the center for the South Vietnamese government. It was also where the USA had its embassy. This was attacked by the Viet Cong in the early morning of January 30, 1968, as part of the Tet Offensive. All the attackers were killed at the time, for the loss of three American lives.

▼ Shell holes dot the front of the U.S. Embassy in Saigon following an attack during the Tet Offensive.

June 5, 1969
American warplanes begin bombing North Vietnam once again.

December 31, 1969
The number of American troops in Vietnam drops below 500,000.

March 1970
American and South Vietnamese forces increase operations in Cambodia (see page 45).

May 9, 1970
Up to 100,000 people protest in Washington, D.C., against the American actions in Cambodia.

The Tet Offensive

On January 30, 1968, NVA troops in North Vietnam launched the Tet Offensive—a huge attack on South Vietnam. At the same time, Viet Cong units began hundreds of raids in towns and cities across the country, even in Saigon. The Americans and South Vietnamese were taken completely by surprise, and had to fight for survival.

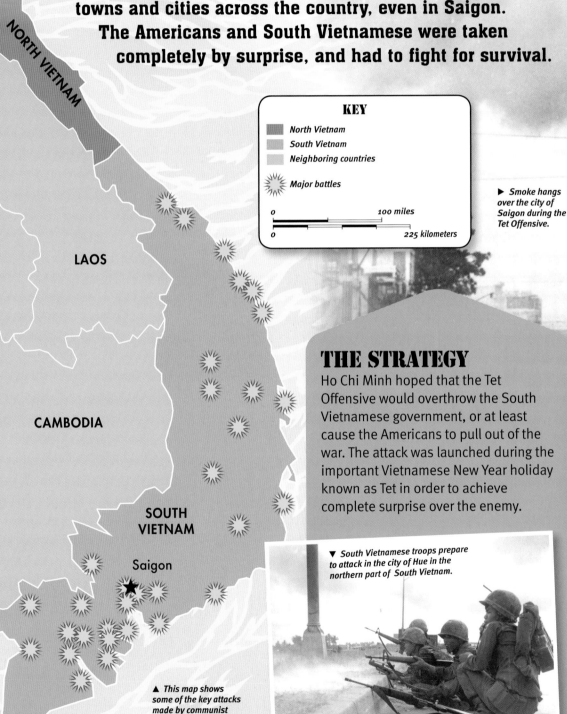

NORTH VIETNAM

LAOS

CAMBODIA

SOUTH VIETNAM

Saigon

KEY

North Vietnam
South Vietnam
Neighboring countries

Major battles

0   100 miles
0   225 kilometers

▶ Smoke hangs over the city of Saigon during the Tet Offensive.

THE STRATEGY

Ho Chi Minh hoped that the Tet Offensive would overthrow the South Vietnamese government, or at least cause the Americans to pull out of the war. The attack was launched during the important Vietnamese New Year holiday known as Tet in order to achieve complete surprise over the enemy.

▼ South Vietnamese troops prepare to attack in the city of Hue in the northern part of South Vietnam.

▲ This map shows some of the key attacks made by communist forces during the Tet Offensive.

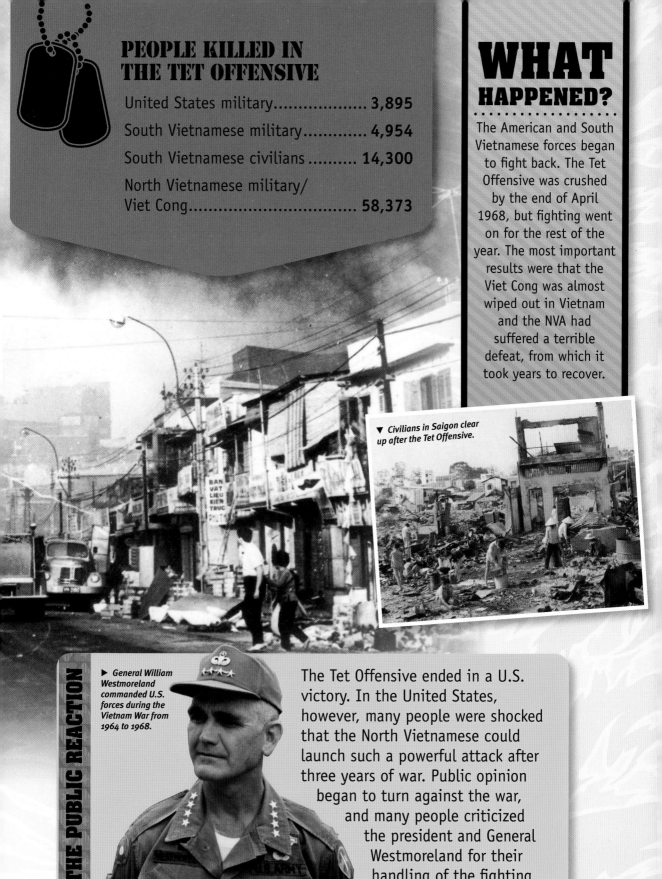

PEOPLE KILLED IN THE TET OFFENSIVE

United States military	3,895
South Vietnamese military	4,954
South Vietnamese civilians	14,300
North Vietnamese military/ Viet Cong	58,373

WHAT HAPPENED?

The American and South Vietnamese forces began to fight back. The Tet Offensive was crushed by the end of April 1968, but fighting went on for the rest of the year. The most important results were that the Viet Cong was almost wiped out in Vietnam and the NVA had suffered a terrible defeat, from which it took years to recover.

▼ Civilians in Saigon clear up after the Tet Offensive.

THE PUBLIC REACTION

▶ General William Westmoreland commanded U.S. forces during the Vietnam War from 1964 to 1968.

The Tet Offensive ended in a U.S. victory. In the United States, however, many people were shocked that the North Vietnamese could launch such a powerful attack after three years of war. Public opinion began to turn against the war, and many people criticized the president and General Westmoreland for their handling of the fighting.

23 The Battle of Khe Sanh

Khe Sanh was a huge U.S. military base in South Vietnam, near the border with Laos. It was held by 6,000 U.S. Marines plus some special forces soldiers. Fighting began around the base on January 20, 1968, but then on February 8 the NVA launched a major attack. Khe Sanh found itself surrounded and under siege for 77 days.

▼ Troops at an FSB cover their ears while firing a large artillery gun.

FIRE SUPPORT BASES

The American forces had bases scattered throughout Vietnam. One of the most important types was the Fire Support Base (**FSB**). This was a base that had artillery guns, which could fire against enemy soldiers in the surrounding area. Soldiers outside the FSB could "call in" artillery fire by talking to the FSB headquarters on their radios.

WHAT HAPPENED?

✹ During the 77-day siege, the Americans at Khe Sanh were surrounded by up to 40,000 NVA troops.

✹ Aircraft brought in supplies and new troops, and many aircraft were destroyed or damaged as they flew into the airfield under enemy fire.

✹ In the end, the NVA was not able to take the base, and they suffered terrible casualties from U.S. bombing and the defenders' fire. The siege officially ended on April 8.

▼ U.S. soldiers walk past a huge pile of used shell casings during the Siege of Khe Sanh.

▼ A U.S. transport plane comes under heavy fire as it takes off from Khe Sanh during the siege.

THE EXPERIENCE OF KHE SANH

Soldiers trapped at Khe Sanh experienced fighting or bombing every day. They constantly had to defend the base against being overrun by the enemy. At night, the NVA launched attacks, which could end up with American and North Vietnamese soldiers fighting hand-to-hand in bunkers and trenches.

▼ A three-man U.S. Marine sniper team spots targets at Khe Sanh.

TO THE RESCUE

Operation *Pegasus*, to relieve the besieged men, was launched on April 1. After heavy fighting, it finally reached the trapped base on April 8. Three days later, the base was once again declared open to the outside world. The siege was over.

▶ Troops march toward Khe Sanh as part of the U.S. relief effort in April 1968.

The Battle of Hue

The ancient city of Hue lay in the northern part of South Vietnam. It was a major target for the forces of the NVA during the Tet Offensive. In the weeks leading up to the offensive, thousands of Viet Cong moved into the city dressed as civilians.

▼ *A marine medic treats a wounded colleague during the battle for Hue.*

WHAT HAPPENED?

● On January 31, 1968, the NVA and VC attacked Hue, and succeeded in taking over most of the city.

● U.S. and South Vietnamese forces counter-attacked, but it took almost four weeks for the city to be captured.

● The battle was fought at close range across streets and within houses. By the time the battle ended, the Americans and ARVN had suffered 668 troops killed, but the NVA had lost more than 5,000 men.

CIVILIANS IN THE WAY

Half of the city of Hue was destroyed in the fighting, and 140,000 people were made homeless. Some 5,000 people had also been executed by the communists.

▶ *Civilians in Hue try to escape the fighting in February 1968. Hundreds were killed by both American and communist fire.*

Helicopter war

▲ *A helicopter carrying Vietnamese evacuees on the deck of U.S.S.* Midway *in 1975.*

MEDICAL EVACUATION

Helicopters were used as flying ambulances in the Vietnam War. To pick up a wounded soldier they would either land on clear ground, or lower a winch down through the jungle and lift the casualty on board. It was dangerous work, but nearly 373,000 wounded soldiers were lifted between 1965 and 1968.

The U.S. and South Vietnamese forces used thousands of helicopters during the Vietnam War. Helicopters were useful for transporting troops and supplies to remote parts of the Vietnamese countryside, and for rescuing wounded soldiers. Some helicopters were also heavily armed with rockets and machine guns, and used for attacking the enemy.

▼ *A U.S. Army Bell Huey helicopter airlifts infantry troops during a search and destroy mission near Cu Chi, South Vietnam, in 1966.*

BELL UH-1

The Bell *UH-1* helicopter was one of the most important helicopters of the Vietnam War. It could carry 14 men or six stretchers, and flew at speeds of 135 miles per hour. Some were also equipped with weapons, such as rocket pods. The *UH-1* was known by the nickname "Huey."

▲ *A South Vietnam Air Force Huey, armed with rocket launchers and machine guns.*

The USA deployed about 12,000 helicopters in the war, of which 3,305 were destroyed.

41

Protests in the USA

The war in Vietnam was unpopular with large numbers of the American public. Many people felt that the goals of the war were not worth the deaths of so many American soldiers and Vietnamese people. Some also disagreed with the destructive tactics used by U.S. forces, which often resulted in the deaths of South Vietnamese civilians. Huge protest marches became common throughout the cities of the United States.

▲ U.S. marshals arrest a protester during a 1967 anti-Vietnam protest in Washington, D.C.

NOVEMBER 27, 1965 WASHINGTON, D.C. UP TO 20,000	MARCH 25–26, 1966 NEW YORK 25,000	OCTOBER 21, 1967 WASHINGTON, D.C. 100,000
1965	**1966**	**1967**

MAJOR ANTI-VIETNAM WAR PROTESTS

▼ Throughout the late 1960s, the number of anti-war protesters grew each year until there were hundreds of thousands in the United States.

THE KENT STATE MASSACRE

Universities and colleges were often centers of protest against the war. On May 4, 1970, soldiers from the Ohio National Guard were called to control a large student protest at Kent State University, Ohio. At one point, the soldiers opened fire with their weapons for 13 seconds. Four students were killed and nine wounded. The killings created even more protests around the United States, and four million students went on strike.

▲ The bell at Kent State University was rung to start the protest, and is today rung every year on the anniversary of the tragedy.

MUHAMMAD ALI

Muhammad Ali was the most famous boxer in the world during the 1960s and 70s. On April 28, 1967, he was served with a draft notice by the U.S. Army, but refused to serve in the Vietnam War. He was sentenced to five years in prison, although he managed to stay out of jail. He was also fined $10,000 and was banned from boxing for three years.

▶ Ali was one of the most famous anti-war protesters.

OCTOBER 15, 1969
WASHINGTON, D.C.
250,000

APRIL 24, 1970
SAN FRANCISCO
156,000

MAY 20, 1970
LOS ANGELES
30,000

1968   1969   1970

MAY 9, 1970
WASHINGTON, D.C.
100,000

In November 1968, Richard Nixon won the election for President of the United States, and began his administration in January 1969. One of the election promises Nixon made was to start withdrawing U.S. troops from Vietnam. He began to do this in 1969, and by the end of 1973 almost all U.S. soldiers were gone from Vietnam.

▼ *Richard Nixon makes a "V" for "victory" sign during his campaign to become President in July 1968.*

NIXON'S PLANS

Nixon had very different ideas from his predecessor about how to deal with the spread of communism. As well as encouraging the South Vietnamese to take over the fighting of the war, he tried to improve relations with the Soviet Union and China. In 1972, his meeting with the Soviet leader Leonid Brezhnev led to a treaty limiting the use of nuclear arms. The same year he spoke to Chinese leader Mao Zedong about ending the war in Vietnam.

NIXON'S KEY IDEAS FOR VIETNAM

* Withdraw all American combat troops.

* Provide supplies and training to South Vietnam, to enable the country to fight the war on its own.

* Attack NVA supply routes in Cambodia.

* Keep pressure on North Vietnam to stop the war.

▲ *Nixon justified the attack on Cambodia as a response to North Vietnamese aggression.*

War in Cambodia

▲ The U.S. 11th Armored Cavalry enters Cambodia in May 1970.

In March 1970, President Nixon ordered secret bombing operations in Cambodia. He wanted to destroy North Vietnamese supply lines and bases in Cambodia, but soon discovered that bombing would not be enough. He felt it was necessary to invade Cambodian territory.

▲ A U.S. soldier reads the military newspaper Stars and Stripes during the Cambodian campaign.

WHAT HAPPENED?

● In April 1970, both South Vietnamese and American forces made large raids into Cambodia. Their purpose was to cut enemy supply routes, destroy bases, and capture communist weapons and equipment.

● At first the operations were successful, but the communists moved back into place as soon as the Americans and South Vietnamese left.

● The invasions were unpopular with many people in the United States, who felt that the war was escalating rather than winding down.

KHMER ROUGE

As well as dealing with the attacks by the South Vietnamese and Americans, the Cambodian government was also fighting a war against communists at this time. The Cambodian communist forces were called the Khmer Rouge, and in 1975 they had taken over much of the country and had the capital, Phnom Penh, surrounded. As the Khmer Rouge troops closed in, the USA launched Operation *Eagle Pull* to airlift its embassy staff and some Cambodian officials to safety.

◄ Pol Pot was a Cambodian revolutionary who ruled the country with great brutality from 1975 to 1979.

About 25 percent of Cambodia's population died as a result of Pol Pot's cruel policies.

Every day, the Vietnam War was brought into people's homes via television, newspapers, magazines, and radio reports. People were able to see for themselves the horror of war as they had never seen it before. Journalists were allowed to go on combat missions with the troops, and brought back dramatic reports and photographs. American citizens were also able to witness the death and injury of American soldiers and South Vietnamese civilians, and this had a major effect on public opinion.

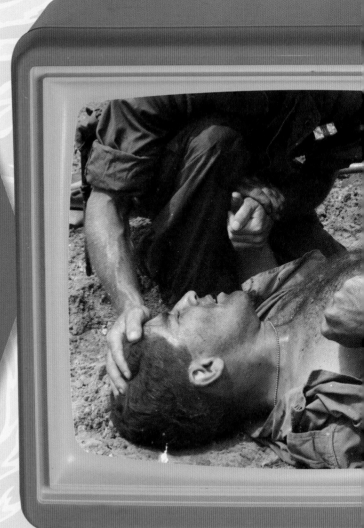

THE INFLUENCE OF TELEVISION

During World War II, war reports were usually seen at the cinema. By the time of the Vietnam War, however, most households in America had a TV set. They could watch television news footage of Vietnam fighting every day. By the early 1970s, satellite broadcasting had also been invented. Pictures were broadcast to the United States from Japan just hours after they were taken.

▶ Television footage of U.S casualties, such as this marine injured by a Viet Cong booby trap in 1968, began to change the public's view of the war.

Between 1955 and 1975, a total of 63 reporters were killed in the Vietnam War.

FAMOUS VIETNAM PHOTOJOURNALISTS

Photojournalists took amazing photographs that often caused a huge amount of discussion back home. Some famous Vietnam photojournalists were:

Don McCullin
A British photographer who worked alongside U.S. Marines during the battle of Hue.

Larry Burrows
Another British photojournalist who covered the Vietnam War from 1962 until 1971. He was killed when the helicopter he was in was shot down; three other photojournalists died with him.

Sean Flynn
This former American actor became a photojournalist in 1966. He covered several wars, including Vietnam, but disappeared in Cambodia. People think he was executed by the Khmer Rouge.

Dicky Chapelle
A female American war correspondent who worked in World War II as well as the Vietnam War, she was killed by a Viet Cong booby trap in November 1965.

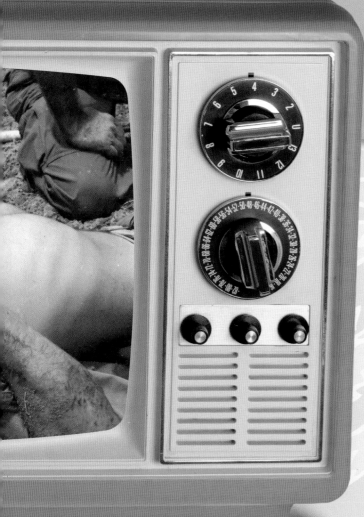

WALTER CRONKITE

▲ *Walter Cronkite delivers one of his famous television addresses. He had visited Vietnam.*

Walter Cronkite was a U.S. journalist and TV broadcaster. During the Vietnam War he became known as "the most trusted man on television," because of his honesty and intelligence. Following the Tet Offensive, he turned against the idea that America was winning the war.

U.S. special forces

Special forces are soldiers who have been trained and equipped to perform the most dangerous missions, often deep in enemy territory. Under President John F. Kennedy, the number of special forces soldiers grew significantly from 1961 onward. During the Vietnam War, these soldiers were used in many different types of operations, from secretly observing the enemy to raiding Viet Cong bases.

◄ U.S. special forces abseil into a South Vietnam conflict zone from a UH-1 Huey helicopter in 1967.

THE SPECIAL OPERATIONS FORCES

There were several varieties of special forces soldier. Some belonged to the U.S. Army special forces—these soldiers were known as the "Green Berets," after the color of their military caps. Some Green Berets joined the Military Assistance Command, Vietnam Special Operations Group (MACV-SOG), a very secretive unit that performed operations in North Vietnam, Laos, and Cambodia. The Central **Intelligence** Agency (CIA) also conducted secret operations in South Vietnam against suspected Viet Cong leaders and informants.

◄ Dressed in camouflage gear, a U.S. special forces soldier keeps guard with a light machine gun in 1968.

▼ Female volunteers in the People's Self-Defense Force, a group that patrolled local villages to protect them from Viet Cong attacks.

◄ A U.S. soldier oversees a shooting practice session with South Vietnamese troops.

TYPICAL SPECIAL FORCES MISSIONS

Special forces used various methods to perform their missions. Their role was to:

★ **TRAIN:** Vietnamese civilians and troops to fight

★ **RESCUE:** U.S. airmen shot down behind enemy lines

★ **ATTACK AND DESTROY:** Viet Cong and NVA bases

★ **DESTROY MILITARY TARGETS:** in North Vietnam, Laos, and Cambodia

★ **GATHER INFORMATION:** on enemy defenses

HEARTS AND MINDS

The U.S. special forces didn't just fight the enemy. Many spent time living in Vietnamese villages and getting to know the people. These missions were known as "hearts and minds" operations, because they were meant to win over the trust of the locals. Some special forces soldiers were trained as veterinarians to treat villagers' animals. Others provided medical care to the people, including vaccinations.

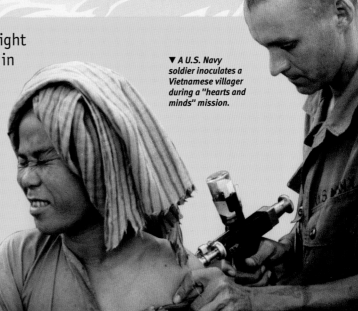

▼ A U.S. Navy soldier inoculates a Vietnamese villager during a "hearts and minds" mission.

The bombing of Laos

Large sections of the Ho Chi Minh Trail ran through the country of Laos, which was heavily bombed by the U.S. Air Force. In fact, Laos would become one of the most bombed countries in history.

◄ Today, more than 40 years after the end of the war, rusted bombs still lie in the jungles and fields of Laos.

LAOS BOMBING STATISTICS

Total days Laos was bombed 2,290

Estimated number of bombs dropped on Laos .... 280 million

Estimated number of bombs that didn't explode..................... 80 million

Amount of money spent per day bombing Laos .... $17 million

Laotians killed or wounded 30,000

NAPALM

A napalm bomb was a special device used in Vietnam. Instead of explosive, it was filled with a jelly-like gasoline. When it was dropped and ignited, the napalm created a huge fireball and burned large areas of ground to ashes. It also stuck to surfaces as it burned, making it lethal to people.

► A U.S. fighter plane drops a napalm bomb over the jungle.

Vietnamization

Vietnamization was President Nixon's bid to make South Vietnam responsible for fighting the war as U.S. troops withdrew. The plan involved enlarging South Vietnam's forces and giving them better weapons. Yet despite U.S. efforts, the South's forces remained outclassed, and much of the aid was wasted through corruption.

▼ *A U.S. soldier trains a South Vietnamese force known as Civilian Irregular Defense Group.*

THE GROWTH OF ARVN

Vietnamization resulted in a massive growth in the size of the ARVN. At the beginning of 1970, the ARVN had about 850,000 men. By 1973, the total size of the South Vietnamese ground forces was in the region of 1 million.

AMERICAN SUPPORT

During the years when Nixon's Vietnamization policy was in effect, huge amounts of military hardware were exported. In total, the United States supplied South Vietnam with more than 500 combat aircraft, 2,000 artillery guns, 12,000 M60 machine guns, 40,000 M79 grenade launchers, and more than 1 million M16 rifles.

▲ *South Vietnamese troops train with a machine gun aboard a U.S.-built armored personnel carrier.*

The ARVN had a high desertion rate—many soldiers left to be closer to their families.

1970–1973

The American withdrawal

The withdrawal of American troops from Vietnam increased during the early 1970s. By 1973, virtually all ground combat troops had gone, and the responsibility for fighting the communists was passed to the South Vietnamese. At the same time, the United States was negotiating with North Vietnam for an end to the war.

▲ Protesters call for Nixon to be impeached (officially charged with a crime) over Watergate.

WATERGATE SCANDAL

In 1973, President Richard Nixon was investigated for his involvement in a 1972 criminal break-in at the Democratic Party's offices in the Watergate Hotel, Washington, D.C. This investigation became known as the "Watergate Scandal." Nixon was forced to resign in 1974 because of the scandal.

▶ Nixon speaks at a press conference during the Watergate Scandal.

Watergate made many people even more unhappy with the way the war was going.

KEY EVENTS

April 4, 1970
About 15,000 people march in Washington, D.C., supporting the U.S. war in Vietnam.

June 29, 1970
American soldiers withdraw from Cambodia.

February 8, 1971
Operation *Lam Son 719* is launched (see page 53).

March 25, 1971
Lam Son 719 ends in failure (see page 53).

LAM SON 719

On February 8, 1971, about 20,000 ARVN soldiers invaded Laos in an attempt to cut North Vietnamese supply lines. The mission was called Operation *Lam Son 719*. U.S. troops provided artillery and air support, but they were not allowed to step inside Laos itself. Although the ARVN mission began well, within two weeks the action was crushed by the NVA. The South Vietnamese troops were forced to retreat, with half of them dead or wounded. It was not a good sign for the future.

▼ *U.S. attack helicopters fly over Laos in Operation Lam Son 719 in 1971.*

◄ *An Australian soldier carries a loaded M60 machine gun in South Vietnam.*

KEY

North Vietnam
South Vietnam
Neighboring countries

◄ ARVN soldiers

0   200 miles

0   400 kilometers

NORTH VIETNAM

LAOS

SOUTH VIETNAM

AUSTRALIA AND NEW ZEALAND

The countries of Australia and New Zealand also sent troops to the Vietnam War. Australia began sending troops in 1962, and about 60,000 Australians had served in the war by 1972. A total of 521 were killed in action. New Zealand is a small country, but still sent 3,000 soldiers and civilians to Vietnam.

August 18, 1971
Australia and New Zealand announce that they are withdrawing all troops from Vietnam.

March 30, 1972
NVA launches the Easter Offensive against South Vietnam (see page 58).

August 12, 1972
The last American ground troops leave Vietnam (see page 63).

January 23, 1973
The USA and North Vietnam sign an agreement to end the war (see page 62).

Riverine war

In 1967, the Americans in Vietnam created the Mobile Riverine Force (MRF). The MRF had hundreds of river boats crewed by men from the U.S. Navy, Army, and Coast Guard. These boats were heavily armed and their job was to fight the Viet Cong in the watery Mekong Delta.

THE MEKONG DELTA

The Mekong Delta covered much of the southern part of South Vietnam. It was an area laced with thousands of miles of rivers, canals, streams, and ditches, all surrounded by jungle or rice paddies. It was a secretive world that the Viet Cong used to move supplies and weapons by boat.

▼ A U.S. river boat uses a flamethrower against enemy positions located on the banks of a river.

▶ A helicopter gunship escorts armed patrol boats along the brown waters of the Mekong Delta.

BROWN WATER NAVY

The MRF was known as the "Brown Water Navy." They were called this because of the color of the water in the Mekong Delta. They would stop and search Vietnamese boats for weapons and supplies for the enemy and take special forces units on raids. They would also use flamethrowers, mortars, and machine guns to destroy enemy bases on the riverbanks.

Capable of reaching speeds of over 35 mph, PCFs were also known as "Swift boats."

▶ The U.S. Navy also used aircraft, such as this Martin P5M Marlin, to patrol the coastline.

The U.S. Navy and Coast Guard also patrolled South Vietnam's coastline. In Operation *Market Time*, more than 600 American boats and warships were active, stopping suspicious vessels or firing on those that didn't stop. They worked alongside special aircraft that used radar and cameras to spot enemy boats. Between 1965 and 1972, the *Market Time* operation stopped 48 North Vietnamese trawlers attempting to take supplies to the South.

▲ These three boats are (from left to right) a PBR (Patrol Boat, River), a PCF (Patrol Craft Fast), and an armored gunboat or monitor.

THE AMERICAN BOATS

The U.S. Navy used different types of boat for different roles.

● PBR—Patrol Boat, River: This boat was designed to float even in very shallow waters and it had a four-man crew.

● PCF—Patrol Craft Fast: This boat was made for speed. As well as weapons, it had a powerful searchlight on board to light up suspicious boats at night.

● Monitor—This had a crew of more than 10 men and was fitted with heavy weaponry, including flamethrowers.

● ASPB—Assault Support Patrol Boat: This was a large boat with five crew members. It was armed with machine guns and was designed to survive underwater explosions.

55

B-52 operations

The **B-52** *Stratofortress* was one of the America's most powerful military airplanes. This giant had eight jet engines and could carry more than 100 bombs weighing up to 70,000 pounds. **B-52s** would fly from the island of Guam, bomb enemy targets in Vietnam, then fly back to base. They were first used against North Vietnam in 1965.

LINEBACKER II

Linebacker II was a *B-52* bombing operation against North Vietnam in late 1972. Its aim was to force North Vietnam back into peace talks. In total, 741 *B-52* missions were flown, dropping 15,237 tons of bombs. Fifteen *B-52s* were shot down. Privately, President Nixon admitted that the operation achieved "zilch."

▶ *Rows of 750-pound bombs are ready to be loaded onto a B-52 Stratofortress in Guam.*

EXPLOSIVES A

B-52 SPECIFICATIONS

Crew: 5
Length: 159 feet 4 inches
Wingspan: 185 feet
Engines: Eight Pratt & Whitney turbofans
Range: 10,000 miles

Speed: 650 miles per hour
Cruise speed: 525 miles per hour
Bombload: 70,000 pounds

Under Project "Big Belly," *B-52s* were modified to carry 27 tons of bombs.

The Phoenix Program

The Phoenix Program was an operation to identify important Viet Cong people in South Vietnam. It was run between 1965 and 1972 by the CIA alongside special forces and South Vietnamese intelligence units. When Viet Cong operators were identified, they were arrested, persuaded to change sides, or killed.

THE CIA

The Central Intelligence Agency (CIA) is a huge intelligence organization in the United States. It was created in 1947, and during the Vietnam War it conducted many secret operations in Vietnam. Its main role was to gather information on the Viet Cong.

◀ A U.S. soldier captures a suspected Viet Cong member during a search and clear mission.

In Vietnam, the CIA operated a fake airline company called "Air America."

TORTURE CAMPAIGN

When Viet Cong operators were captured, they were often taken to South Vietnamese **interrogation** centers, where many were tortured for information. In total, 81,740 people were taken in the Phoenix Program, and 26,369 were killed.

▼ U.S. troops guard blindfolded Viet Cong prisoners during Operation Starlite, a major offensive in 1965.

▲ Vietnamese villagers arrested in 1966 by U.S. troops for being suspected communists.

37 ▸ The Easter Offensive

Fighting in Vietnam grew more intense during the first three months of 1972. Yet the North Vietnamese government was planning for final victory. On March 30, it launched a massive invasion of South Vietnam, attacking the country from different directions in order to confuse the ARVN. The North Vietnamese called it the Nguyen Hue Campaign, while the South Vietnamese and Americans called it the Easter Offensive.

NORTH VIETNAM

LAOS

CAMBODIA

SOUTH VIETNAM

★ Saigon

▲ North Vietnamese forces invaded South Vietnam at the same time at three separate points.

KEY

North Vietnam
South Vietnam
Neighboring countries

NVA major attack

0 — 200 miles
0 — 450 kilometers

WHAT HAPPENED?

As the NVA advanced deep into South Vietnam, the Easter Offensive at first seemed successful. Then the United States launched a bombing campaign against North Vietnam called *Linebacker I*, destroying bridges, factories, oil depots, and other important targets. Mines were dropped into North Vietnamese harbors to stop ships coming in. *Linebacker I* was devastating, and it helped ARVN to push the NVA back out of South Vietnam in June.

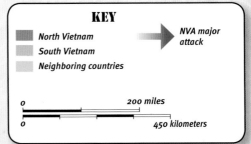

BATTLE OF AN LOC

An Loc was one of the biggest battles of the Vietnam War. It began on April 13, 1972, and lasted for 66 days. The battle resulted in a major victory for ARVN forces, and halted the NVA's advance toward Saigon during the Easter Offensive. The town of An Loc was key to protecting the North's supplies coming from nearby Laos. At the outset of the attack, the single ARVN division stationed there was massively outnumbered by three NVA and Viet Cong divisions and was quickly besieged. The ARVN forces, however, had one huge advantage—they could call upon U.S. air power, including the bombing might of the *B-52 Stratofortress*. With U.S. air support the ARVN were able to repel the NVA's massive tank and artillery attacks. By the end of the battle in May 1972, the U.S. was using every *B-52* it had in Southeast Asia to pound the NVA into giving up.

▲ *The South Vietnamese President Nguyen Van Thieu (right) celebrates with ARVN commanders after the Battle of An Loc.*

▼ *An ARVN soldier observes the devastation during the Battle of Kontum.*

BATTLE OF KONTUM

The city of Kontum was attacked by the NVA on May 14, 1972. NVA forces now had many tanks, which had been supplied by the Soviets. ARVN troops and U.S. helicopter gunships managed to destroy many of these tanks, while *B-52s* hit the enemy troops. The NVA kept attacking, but they couldn't defeat the ARVN defenders. The communist soldiers pulled back on May 31.

Defoliants

▲ In 1972, the U.S. Air Force removed stocks of Agent Orange from Vietnam and destroyed them at Johnston Atoll, near Hawaii.

Defoliants are chemicals designed to strip leaves from trees and kill plants. American aircraft sprayed millions of gallons of a defoliant called Agent Orange over South Vietnam and North Vietnam. The aim was to take away the cover used by enemy troops and also to kill the crops they ate.

OPERATION RANCH HAND

The U.S. defoliation program was called Operation *Ranch Hand* and lasted from 1962 to 1971. During that time, some 19 million gallons of defoliant were sprayed, affecting 4.5 million acres of land, and about 20 percent of South Vietnam's forests.

HEALTH EFFECTS

Agent Orange had serious health effects on people who were exposed to it, including life-threatening illnesses such as cancer. Many babies were born with disabilities because their pregnant mothers came into contact with the chemical. The Vietnamese government claims that 400,000 people were killed or injured from Agent Orange.

Birth deformities caused by Agent Orange include extra fingers and toes.

Drugs and discipline

For American combat soldiers, the Vietnam War was a stressful experience. They had to watch friends die, and were under the constant threat of ambush. Some turned to drugs in an attempt to escape reality. This led to problems with discipline, particularly as the war became unpopular.

MENTAL HEALTH

The Vietnam War saw many veterans return home with a condition called Post-Traumatic Stress Disorder (PTSD). PTSD is caused by experiencing very distressing situations, and can cause nightmares, anxiety, fear, anger, and difficulty in thinking clearly.

▲ U.S. troops taking a break while out on patrol. Many turned to illegal drugs as a way of coping with stress and fatigue.

MY LAI MASSACRE

On March 16, 1968, a unit of U.S. soldiers was under orders to root out Viet Cong in the village of My Lai, South Vietnam. But the discipline of the under-pressure soldiers totally broke down, leading to them killing up to 500 civilians, mostly unarmed women, children, and old people. When the killings became known in the USA in 1969, it caused a huge outcry.

▲ A U.S. soldier burns the home of a villager in My Lai along with some reed mats used for drying crops.

There were around 1,000 cases of American officers being attacked by their own men.

Paris peace talks

Peace talks between North Vietnam, South Vietnam, and the United States were held in Paris between 1968 and 1973. Key people were the U.S. National Security Advisor Henry Kissinger and Le Duc Tho, a North Vietnamese diplomat. After five years an agreement was signed.

WHAT WAS AGREED?

★ **CEASEFIRE:** Throughout Vietnam, beginning at 8 a.m., January 28, 1973

★ **U.S. WITHDRAWAL:** All U.S. troops to withdraw in 60 days after the ceasefire

★ **PRISONERS OF WAR:** Both sides to release all their prisoners of war

★ **POLITICAL FUTURE:** South Vietnamese people to be allowed to decide their own political future

★ **REUNIFICATION:** Reunification of Vietnam to be carried out only via peaceful means.

▼ *The United States's growing casualties and North Vietnam's failure in the Easter Offensive led to a breakthrough after years of talks. The agreement was signed on January 27, 1973.*

HENRY KISSINGER

Henry Kissinger was born in Germany, but moved to the United States in 1938. He was a key negotiator during the Vietnam War. He was awarded the Nobel Peace Prize with Le Duc Tho for seeming to bring the war to an end in 1973, and served as Secretary of State until 1977.

◄ *Kissinger spent years trying to find a peace settlement. The North Vietnamese, however, were stil focused on taking over South Vietnam.*

By 1973, the war was so unpopular that Nixon was under huge pressure to make peace.

The departure of U.S. forces

On March 29, 1973, President Nixon withdrew the last American ground troops from South Vietnam. Most of the soldiers went home on troop ships or by passenger aircraft, to begin new lives back in the United States.

MISSING IN ACTION

Although all American troops had left Vietnam in 1973, there were 2,646 U.S. soldiers listed as "Missing in Action" (MIA). This meant that the government had no reliable information about what had happened to them. Since 1975, however, the bodies of more than 1,000 MIA have been found. They were actually killed in battle.

◄ The Prisoners of War/Missing in Action flag was created in 1972 to remind people about missing soldiers in Vietnam and elsewhere.

Remains of U.S. soldiers killed in Vietnam are still being found and sent home to the USA.

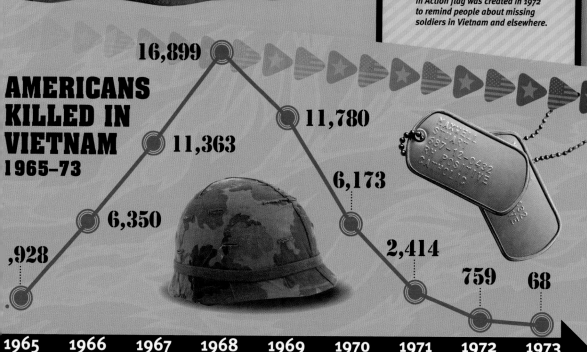

AMERICANS KILLED IN VIETNAM
1965–73

- ,928
- 6,350
- 11,363
- 16,899
- 11,780
- 6,173
- 2,414
- 759
- 68

| 1965 | 1966 | 1967 | 1968 | 1969 | 1970 | 1971 | 1972 | 1973 |

The POW experience

More than 700 Americans became prisoners of war (POWs) of the Viet Cong and the North Vietnamese during the Vietnam War. Almost all were treated very badly. Torture was often used, while many people were kept totally alone in small, dirty rooms. Sometimes this treatment would go on for many years.

Torture was often used to try to convert U.S. prisoners of war to communism.

◄ *POWs stare out through the bars at the Hanoi Hilton.*

HANOI HILTON

The *"Hanoi Hilton"* was the name Americans jokingly used for the Hoa Lo prison in Hanoi. ("Hilton" is the name of a popular luxury hotel chain). The prisoners were kept in terrible cells. These were filthy, extremely hot in the summer, and very cold in the winter. The food was awful, and often had insects wriggling in it. Prisoners managed to talk to one another by tapping coded messages on the prison's walls and water pipes.

▲ Armed U.S. soldiers sit inside a helicopter on their way to raid the Son Tay prison camp.

SON TAY RAID

On November 21, 1970, 56 U.S. special forces soldiers raided the Son Tay prison camp in North Vietnam. Their mission was to rescue up to 500 American prisoners believed to be held there. The mission went as planned and the camp was captured, but the troops found that the prisoners had already been moved.

▶ The North Vietnamese treated McCain's injuries only when they learned that his father was a top admiral. McCain's capture made headline news in the United States.

JOHN McCAIN

John McCain is a U.S. Senator, but during the Vietnam War he was a combat pilot. He was shot down over North Vietnam in October 1967, and was captured by the North Vietnamese. Despite having a broken leg and two broken arms, he was treated very badly. He was held prisoner for five and a half years, and was tortured and spent two years in solitary confinement (entirely on his own in a room). He was finally released on March 14, 1973.

OPERATION HOMECOMING

American prisoners were finally returned to the United States from North Vietnam in 1973. In what became known as Operation *Homecoming*, 591 prisoners were released. They were flown home on 54 aircraft flights, known as the "Hanoi Taxi." Each plane brought home 40 men. Some had been held captive for eight years.

▲ Released U.S. POWs celebrate aboard a "Hanoi Taxi" en route to Clark Air Base in the Philippines, in March 1973.

1974–1975

Defeat in South Vietnam

Only months after the Paris Peace Accords, North Vietnam renewed its attacks on the South. In April 1975, South Vietnam's capital, Saigon, fell to the communists. President Nguyen Van Thieu fled, as did all the remaining Americans. It was a terrible defeat for South Vietnam after so many years of war and hundreds of thousands of people killed.

Vietnam continued to fight border conflicts with its neighbors until 1991.

▶ *The remains of an American M-14 tank destroyed by a mine near Chu Chi.*

KEY EVENTS

January 4, 1974	**August 5, 1974**	**April 15, 1975**	**April 17, 1975**
President Thieu states that the Vietnam War has recommenced (see page 67).	The U.S. Congress limits the amount of aid to South Vietnam (see page 67).	North Vietnamese successes mean they are now just 40 miles from Saigon (see page 68).	In Cambodia, the capital Phnom Penh is captured by the Khmer Rouge (see page 45).

AN AMERICAN DEFEAT?

Many still argue about whether the United States was defeated in the Vietnam War. The U.S. military was certainly not defeated. In every battle the Americans fought with the Viet Cong or the NVA, the Americans won. Yet the war became so unpopular with the American public that the United States pulled out. With the Americans gone, South Vietnam was not able to fight off the communist forces.

▲ Thieu fled to Taiwan as North Vietnamese forces entered Saigon.

NGUYEN VAN THIEU

Elected president of South Vietnam in 1967, Thieu signed the Paris Peace Accords in 1973 very reluctantly. He thought the North Vietnamese would break the agreement and the USA would leave his country to its fate. When North Vietnam did attack again, Thieu announced in January 1974 that the war had recommenced.

▶ Senator Frank Church was a long-standing opponent of the war. In 1973, he secured the Case–Church Amendment, which prohibited further U.S. military action unless the president first obtained the approval of Congress.

BROKEN PROMISES

As part of the peace deal, the United States had promised to provide military help to South Vietnam if the North attacked again. But when the NVA did restart its offensive, the U.S. Congress refused to keep funding the conflict knowing how unpopular the war was with the public. President Thieu resigned, claiming that the United States had not kept its word.

April 21, 1975
President Thieu resigns. Duong Van Minh takes over (see page 70).

April 30, 1975
The U.S. embassy in Saigon is evacuated. Communist troops enter the city (see page 70).

July 2, 1976
North and South Vietnam merge. Many in the South are sent to "re-education camps" (see page 70).

1978–1980
Thousands of "boat people" flee communist rule in Vietnam (see page 73).

The last invasion

By March 1974, the NVA had moved 185,000 troops and 700 tanks into South Vietnam, in violation of the Paris Peace Accords. South Vietnamese soldiers were being killed in large numbers. It became obvious that the NVA would soon march on Saigon and capture the country.

◀ *A North Vietnamese invasion of the Central Highlands in March 1975 took the South by surprise, and opened the route to Saigon.*

WHAT HAPPENED?

The NVA launched major offensives in December 1974. By January 6, 1975, the city of Phuoc Long had been captured. This town was just 75 miles from Saigon. The NVA also fought and won hard battles in the Central Highlands of South Vietnam. By the middle of April, communist troops were only 40 miles from Saigon and 200,000 NVA forces were occupying much of the country.

The ARVN retreated in a journey that became known as the "column of tears."

NORTH VIETNAM

SOUTH VIETNAM

Saigon ★

KEY

North Vietnam

South Vietnam

Central Highlands

0   150 miles

0   300 kilometers

▲ *The ARVN's retreat was slowed by ruined roads and bridges.*

COMPARING THE FORCES

	NORTH VIETNAM (NVA)	SOUTH VIETNAM (ARVN)
WEAPONS	Modern Soviet weapons	Modern American weapons
SOLDIERS	375,000	662,000
LEADERSHIP	Very confident political and military leaders	A lot of corruption and poor leadership
SUPPORT	Financial and military support from the Soviet Union	U.S. financial support reduced in October 1974, weakening the South Vietnamese military
MORALE	The communist troops were excited about the coming victory	Many South Vietnamese soldiers were demoralized by their situation

▲ *Some fortunate refugees were evacuated from Saigon by air. In Operation Babylift, more than 3,000 children were evacuated to the United States and other countries before the fall of Saigon.*

REFUGEES

As the communist forces spread throughout South Vietnam, hundreds of thousands of civilians left their homes and swarmed into Saigon. They had only the belongings they could carry, and many were ill or injured. Although they hoped to be rescued, few were.

The fall of Saigon

In the last week of April 1975, the NVA forces advanced to the very edge of Saigon. By April 28, they were just 3 miles from the center of the city, by which time U.S. helicopters and aircraft were evacuating hundreds of people. President Thieu had resigned on April 21, and was replaced by General Duong Van Minh, but he was only to serve two days as President.

TAKING OVER THE CITY

On the morning of April 30, President Minh told his soldiers in Saigon to stop fighting. By midday the communists had taken over the city. NVA tanks actually smashed through the gates of the presidential palace to take Minh's surrender. The Vietnam War was finally over.

▼ *North Vietnamese tanks roll through the gates of the presidential palace in Saigon on April 30, 1975.*

COMMUNIST RE-EDUCATION

After their victory, the communist forces set up "re-education" camps. These were basically prisons for people who the communists considered a threat to their society. Possibly more than 2 million people were held in these camps, and conditions were so bad that as many as 165,000 died.

The final American evacuation

Although most American soldiers had left Vietnam by 1975, there were still some American government workers and troops in Saigon as the communists approached. They, and certain South Vietnamese people and their families, needed to be evacuated quickly.

▼ Hundreds of Americans and Vietnamese are offloaded onto U.S.S. Midway during Operation Frequent Wind.

The *CH-53 Sea Stallion* helicopter used in Saigon could lift up to 55 people at a time.

OPERATION FREQUENT WIND

The evacuation mission was called Operation *Frequent Wind*. Over a period of 19 hours, 81 U.S. helicopters flew frantically in and out of Saigon, taking people to safety aboard ships waiting off the coast. More than 1,000 Americans were rescued.

VIETNAMESE EVACUATION

As well as the Americans, 6,000 Vietnamese citizens were also rescued in Operation *Frequent Wind*. Other civilians set out to sea in small boats, and forced some American ships to pick them up before they sailed away.

◄ Evacuees climb up toward a helicopter on a Saigon rooftop as NVA troops march on the city.

▼ Vietnamese refugees arrive by helicopter on a U.S. aircraft carrier.

The NVA often used mines designed to blow off just a foot or leg, but not to kill the person.

More than 300,000 soldiers were wounded in Vietnam. Injuries varied from small cuts to entire legs or arms being blown off. In total, 5,283 men went home missing one or more limbs. They faced a difficult period in their lives as they tried to adjust to civilian life.

TOP CAUSES OF INJURY FOR U.S. SOLDIERS

+ 1. ARTILLERY SHELLS
+ 2. BULLETS
+ 3. BOOBY TRAPS AND MINES

◄ A U.S. Navy nurse checks the condition of a wounded soldier at a field hospital in Da Nang, South Vietnam in 1968.

WALTER REED HOSPITAL

Once wounded veterans were moved back from South Vietnam to the United States, many were medically treated in the Walter Reed Army Medical Center (WRAMC). This was located in Washington, D.C., and it handled tens of thousands of soldiers from 1903 until 2011.

▶ The Walter Reed facility treated more than 150,000 active and retired personnel from all branches of the military.

Vietnam after the war

In 1976, North and South Vietnam officially became one country, called the Socialist Republic of Vietnam. Hanoi was made the capital of the country, and Saigon was renamed Ho Chi Minh City. The country soon found itself fighting a new war, this time against Cambodia.

▼ The Tuol Sleng Genocide Museum near Phnom Penh in Cambodia is on the site of a notorious prison where up 20,000 people were killed by the Khmer Rouge regime between 1975 and 1979.

WHAT HAPPENED?

Vietnam and Cambodia had fought each other in the past. Under the cruel communist leader Pol Pot, Cambodia launched raids into Vietnam in the 1970s, and fighting grew in 1975–77. In December 1978, Vietnam launched a massive invasion of Cambodia and quickly removed the Khmer Rouge from power.

Of the 17,000 prisoners held at the Khmer Rouge's Tuol Sleng prison, only 12 survived.

BOAT PEOPLE

From 1978 until the 1990s, about 800,000 people fled Vietnam. They were trying to escape the communist rule, and to find new lives in different countries. The were called the "boat people" because most tried to escape in small boats. Hundreds drowned when their boats sank in the open ocean.

▶ From refugee camps in Southeast Asia most of the boat people were resettled in the United States, Canada, France, and Australia.

Homecoming

Coming home could be difficult for Vietnam veterans. Incidents like the My Lai Massacre meant that veterans sometimes had abuse shouted at them in the street. Some also found it difficult to adjust to civilian life after the experience of combat. Most veterans, however, have said that they felt proud of their service in Vietnam, and have gone on to have successful careers and to raise families.

VIETNAM VETERANS STATISTICS

Number of American soldiers who served in Vietnam: **NEARLY 3 MILLION**

Number of American women who served in Vietnam: 7,500

Average age of Vietnam soldier: 22

▼ Vietnam veterans proudly march during a United States Independence Day parade in Michigan in 2011.

VETERANS AGAINST THE WAR

Some veterans joined the anti-war movement when they returned home, as they wanted to protest against the things they had seen and done in Vietnam. The main organization for them was Vietnam Veterans Against the War (VVAW). During the war it had as many as 25,000 members.

▼ Veterans protest against the Vietnam War in Washington D.C. in 1967.

Legacy

After the war, Vietnam had many hard years ahead of it. It was difficult for many people to find work and make money, so there was a lot of poverty. The communist government tried to change the way farms produced food, but this created terrible food shortages. Vietnam came to depend on the Soviet Union for food. It has taken many years for Vietnam to improve the lives of its citizens.

▼ The Ho Chi Minh Museum in Hanoi honors communist Vietnam's founding father.

UNEXPLODED BOMBS

Vietnam is still littered with unexploded bombs and mines. In 2012 alone, 500 people were killed or injured by Vietnam War bombs going off. Some people actually attempt to collect the bombs, to sell them for scrap metal. Experts think it could take 100 years to clear Vietnam entirely of these bombs.

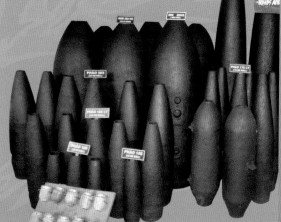

▶ A selection of some of the unexploded bombs dropped during the war.

Today, the United States and Vietnam cooperate peacefully and buy goods from each other.

WHO'S WHO?
The Vietnam War

These are some of the most important political and military figures from the three main participants in the Vietnam War: North Vietnam, South Vietnam, and the United States.

United States

General William Westmoreland

Commander of U.S. forces in Vietnam: 1964–68.
During Westmoreland's term, it was realized that the Vietnam War would not be a quick victory for the USA.

General Creighton Abrams

Commander of U.S. forces in Vietnam: 1968–72.
Under Abrams, U.S. troop numbers decreased, while U.S. aid to South Vietnam's military forces increased.

President John F. Kennedy

President of the United States: 1961–1963.
A fierce anti-communist, Kennedy provided financial aid and military advisors to South Vietnam.

President Lyndon Johnson

President of the United States: 1963–1969.
The conflict increased under Johnson who sent thousands of U.S. troops to fight the NVA and Viet Cong.

President Richard Nixon

President of the United States: 1969–1974.
With the war now unpopular with the American people, Nixon oversaw the withdrawal of U.S troops.

Dr. Henry Kissinger

U.S. National Security Advisor: 1969–1975.
Kissinger helped to negotiate the 1973 peace deal between the USA, North Vietnam, and South Vietnam.

Robert McNamara

Secretary of Defense: 1961–1968.
McNamara resigned in late 1967, believing that the USA's war strategy in Vietnam wasn't working.

Ho Chi Minh

Leader of the Communist Party of Vietnam: 1951–1969.
He also served as Prime Minister, from 1945–55, and President, from 1945–69, of North Vietnam.

Le Duc Tho

North Vietnamese politician
Tho took part in the peace talks with Henry Kissinger that resulted in the Paris Accords of 1973.

QUYẾT THẮNG

North Vietnam

Ngo Dinh Diem

First President of South Vietnam: 1955–1963.
The unpopular Diem was killed by South Vietnam's military leaders, who then took over running the country.

South Vietnam

Vo Nguyen Giap

Commander of North Vietnamese forces: 1945–1981.
He was the main military commander of the NVA both during the Indochina War with France and the Vietnam War.

Nguyen Van Thieu

President of South Vietnam: 1965–1975.
The former general ruled Vietnam until just a few days before it was conquered by North Vietnam.

Duong Van Minh

Last President of South Vietnam: 1975
President for just two days in April 1975, the senior general surrendered to the North Vietnamese forces.

GLOSSARY

ARVN
Army of the Republic of Vietnam (the army of South Vietnam).

ASSASSINATE
To kill a political leader, usually for political reasons.

B-52
A type of large aircraft used by the USA won bombing missions during the Vietnam War—the "B" stands for "bomber."

BOOBY TRAP
A device designed to kill or injure a person when they set it off by accident.

CIA
Central Intelligence Agency. The body that undertakes most of the USA's spying operations overseas.

CIDGS
Civilian Irregular Defense Groups—made up of South Vietnamese villagers trained to fight the communists.

COMMUNISM
A type of politics in which all property is owned by the government, which is made up only of people in the communist party.

DEMOCRACY
A type of politics in which people can own private property and vote for leaders from different political parties.

DMZ
Demilitarized Zone—the area between North Vietnam and South Vietnam that was meant to be free from soldiers.

DRAFTED
To be randomly selected from the U.S. population to serve in the military.

FSB
Fire Support Base—a base that had artillery guns, which could fire against enemy soldiers in the surrounding area.

FRENCH INDOCHINA
A colony owned by France made up of Vietnam, Cambodia, and Laos.

GENEVA ACCORDS
The peace agreement signed in 1954 that brought the Indochina War to an end.

GUERRILLA
A style of warfare using unusual tactics, such as surprise raids and sabotage. The soldiers using these tactics are guerrillas.

HO CHI MINH TRAIL
The communist supply route that ran from North Vietnam into South Vietnam by way of the neighboring countries of Laos and Cambodia.

INTELLIGENCE
Information gathered about the enemy.

INTERROGATION

A method of finding out information via an intense—and often very long—questioning session with a suspect.

MINE

A hidden bomb (usually placed underwater or underground) that explodes when touched.

NVA

North Vietnamese Army—the main military force of North Vietnam.

OFFENSIVE

A military operation designed to gain territory or to achieve a particular outcome or objective.

PHOTOJOURNALIST

A person who takes photographs for stories in magazines and newspapers.

RESOLUTION

An official decision to do something about a situation.

SAM

Surface-to-air missile—a missile used to shoot down airplanes.

SEARCH AND DESTROY

A military tactic used by the USA in Vietnam, which involved seeking out enemy bases and then completely destroying them.

SOVIET UNION

The biggest communist power at the time of the Vietnam war. It was made up of several countries, but centered on Russia.

SPECIAL FORCES

Soldiers who are trained and equipped to do dangerous missions.

SURVEILLANCE

The process of secretly watching people and gathering information about them.

TET

The Vietnamese New Year celebrations in January.

U.S. CONGRESS

The part of the U.S. government that passes laws, made up of the Senate and the House of Representatives.

VIET CONG

The communist fighters operating inside Vietnam—sometimes shortened to VC.

VIET MINH

The communist fighters who fought against the French in the Indochina War in the late 1940s and early 1950s.

VIETNAMIZATION

The American attempt to equip and train the South Vietnamese to fight for themselves against the communists.

INDEX

Picture credits (t=top, b=bottom, l=left, r=right, c=center, fc=front cover, bc=back cover)

All images public domain unless otherwise indicated:
Dreamstime: fc line 1l, line 1r, line 2l, line 3l, line 3lc, line 4lc, line 4rc, line 5l, line 6lc, line 7c, line 7r, 4–5c, 24tr, 33bl, 33br, 46–47, 50tr, 63c, 63cb, 66–67c,
72tr, 75br. *Getty Images*: 70c Herve Gloaguen, 76tl AFP, 76br Howard Sochureck. *Shutterstock.com*: fc line 3 lc. *Wikimedia Commons*: bc cb Hu Totya, 7cl RJT,
8tr Ricardo Stuckert, 17tl Pashtunwarrior, 17tr Michal Mañas, 17tlc Ulmosto, 24 br Paul Mashburn, 25cr Polansky Kolbe, 27tr Bubba73, 27br Tourbillon, 33cr
Richard Bartz, 43cr Jon Ridinger, 43bl Leena Krohn, 47tl Jac de Nijs/Anefo, 63br dog-tag.de, 68b DXLINH, 73c Bjorn Christian Torrissen, 74c Dwight Burdette.